This journal belongs to

_____

If found please return to

- - - - - - - - - - - - - - - - - - - -

Dedicated to mothers and their daughters

When you're caught in the day to day routine,
sometimes it's hard to take time out to connect.
This keepsake journal is designed for just that.
Take time to fill in the questions, to have the
conversations that bring you closer.

Learn new things about each other and have fun!

Follow the instructions on every page.

There are writing prompts, quizzes, bucket lists,
recipes you can share and letters you can write
to each other.

How well do you know your mom?

Put a tick in the box for every answer you get right.

- What's her favourite movie?
- Who was her first love?
- What makes her cry?
- What's her favourite meal?
- What makes her laugh?
- Who is her best friend?
- What does she love to do on a Friday night?
- Is she a cat or dog person?
- Who is her celebrity crush?
- What's her dream car?
- What's her favourite holiday tradition?
- What annoys her most?
- What's her favourite song?
- Does she like to karaoke?
- When is her birthday?
- What's her favourite colour?
- Does she believe in ghosts?
- Is she superstitious?
- Who is her best friend?
- If she was stranded on an island, what would she take with her?
- Who does she love?
- Who does she admire?
- If she could be anywhere in the world, where would she be?
- What's one tv show she could watch over and over again?

How well do you know your daughter?

Put a tick in the box for every answer you get right.

- [ ] What's her favourite movie?
- [ ] Who was her first love?
- [ ] What makes her cry?
- [ ] What's her favourite meal?
- [ ] What makes her laugh?
- [ ] Who is her best friend?
- [ ] What does she love to do on a Friday night?
- [ ] Is she a cat or dog person?
- [ ] Who is her celebrity crush?
- [ ] What's her dream car?
- [ ] What's her favourite holiday tradition?
- [ ] What annoys her most?
- [ ] What's her favourite song?
- [ ] Does she like to karaoke?
- [ ] When is her birthday?
- [ ] What's her favourite colour?
- [ ] Does she believe in ghosts?
- [ ] Is she superstitious?
- [ ] Who is her best friend?
- [ ] If she was stranded on an island, what would she take with her?
- [ ] Who does she love?
- [ ] Who does she admire?
- [ ] If she could be anywhere in the world, where would she be?
- [ ] What's one tv show she could watch over and over again?

FIRSTS & LASTS

MOM	DAUGHTER

When was the first time you fell in love?

When was the last time you fell in love?

Who was it with?

Who was it with?

Conversation starters:

1. Do you believe in love at first sight?
2. What makes you feel loved?
3. What does romance mean to you?

THE DESERT ISLAND

MOM	DAUGHTER

If you were stranded on a desert island and could only bring 3 things, what would they be?

If you were stranded on a desert island and could only bring 3 things, what would they be?

Who would you bring with you?

Who would you bring with you?

Conversation starters:

1. Do you know any survival skills?
2. If you could learn one thing, what would it be?
3. If you had to eat one food for the rest of your life, what would it be?

FRIDAY NIGHTS

MOM	DAUGHTER

Your idea of a fun Friday night is...

Your idea of a fun Friday night is...

What's the best Friday night you've ever had?

What's the best Friday night you've ever had?

Conversation starters:

1. What's the latest you've ever stayed up?
2. What's your favourite day of the week and why?
3. What's something we can do together on a Friday night?

SECRETS! SHHH...

MOM	DAUGHTER

Are you good at keeping secrets?

Are you good at keeping secrets?

What's one thing that many people don't know about you?

What's one thing that many people don't know about you?

Conversation starters:

1. Have you ever spilled the beans on a secret?
2. Who do you share your secrets with?
3. Has there ever been a time where you were afraid to tell me something?

HAVE YOU EVER...

MOM	DAUGHTER

Have you ever been arrested?

Have you ever been arrested?

Have you ever cheated on a test?

Have you ever cheated on a test?

Conversation starters:

1. What's the biggest mistake you've ever made?
2. How do your learn from your mistakes?
3. What's your biggest regret?

CELEBRITIES...

MOM	DAUGHTER

Let's say you could invite 4 famous people to dinner. Who would they be?

Let's say you could invite 4 famous people to dinner. Who would they be?

What would you want to ask them?

What would you want to ask them?

Conversation starters:

1. Tell me about your role models.
2. If you could date any celebrity, who would it be?
3. Have you ever met a celebrity?

BODY BEAUTIFUL...

MOM	DAUGHTER

What do you love most about your body?

What do you love most about your body?

What do you like least about your body?

What do you like least about your body?

Conversation starters:

1. What is your ideal of the perfect body?
2. Would you ever consider plastic surgery?
3. What do you think about the models you see in magazines?

THE MILLIONAIRE
$ QUESTION

MOM	DAUGHTER

What would you do if you won 1 million dollars?

What would you do if you won 1 million dollars?

Who is the first person you'd call if you won the lottery?

Who is the first person you'd call if you won the lottery?

Conversation starters:

1. True or false. The best things in life are free.
2. If you won the lottery, would you continue to work?
3. How much money would you want to win and why?

FEAR FACTORS

MOM	DAUGHTER

What are you the most scared of?

What are you the most scared of?

What is one fear you've had to overcome?

What is one fear you've had to overcome?

Conversation starters:

1. True or false. Fear is a mindset.
2. How do you deal with your fears?
3. When you're scared to do something, would you do it anyway?

YOU & I

MOM	DAUGHTER

What are three things you love about me?

What are three things you love about me?

What can I do to be a better mom?

What can I do to be a better daughter?

Conversation starters:

1. How would you describe our relationship?
2. What can we do to strengthen our bond?
3. What's an activity we can share together?

HEROS

MOM	DAUGHTER

If you could be a super hero, what name would you give yourself?

If you were a super hero, what name would you give yourself?

What would your super power be?

What would your super power be?

Conversation starters:

1. Think of an everyday super hero, who is it?
2. Who do you admire most?
3. What makes a great role model?

HOUSE RULES

MOM	DAUGHTER

If you could re-write the house rules, which one would you change first?

If you could re-write the house rules, which one would you change first?

What's your least favourite house rule?

What's your least favourite house rule?

Conversation starters:

1. What does your dream home look like?
2. What does your dream room look like?
3. If you could have houses around the world, where would they be?

AROUND THE
WORLD

MOM

DAUGHTER

If you could be anywhere in the world right now, where would it be?

If you could be anywhere in the world right now, where would it be?

Do you want to learn a new language?

Do you want to learn a new language?

Conversation starters:

1. Where in the world do you love most?
2. Do you travel with a lot of baggage?
3. If you could collect one thing from all over the world, what would it be?

HOLIDAYS

MOM	DAUGHTER
If you could make up a new holiday, which would it be?	If you could make up a new holiday, which would it be?
What are your favourite holiday traditions?	What are your favourite holiday traditions?

Conversation starters:

1. How would you like to celebrate our next holiday together?
2. What's a new holiday tradition you'd like to start?
3. What's one holiday we don't celebrate enough?

THE WILD LIFE

MOM

DAUGHTER

If you could speak to any animal which would it be?

If you could speak to any animal which would it be?

What would you ask them?

What would you ask them?

Conversation starters:

1. If you made a cave, what would be in it?
2. What would you build your cave from?
3. Who would you invite?

DREAM JOBS

MOM	DAUGHTER

If money wasn't an issue and you could do anything you want, what job would you have?

If money wasn't an issue and you could do anything you want, what job would you have?

What's something you love to do?

What's something you love to do?

Conversation starters:

1. What does it mean to you to be successful?
2. What are a few jobs you'd love to have?
3. What are some jobs you haven't liked?

CHARADES

MOM	DAUGHTER

If you were a character in a movie, which would you play?

If you were a character in a movie, which would you play?

If you could be anyone for the day, who would it be?

If you could be anyone for the day, who would it be?

Conversation starters:

1. Do you have a favourite movie?
2. When was the last time a movie made you cry?
3. What's one movie you can watch over and over again?

DAYDREAMS

MOM	DAUGHTER

What's one thing you always daydream about?

What's one thing you always daydream about?

What's the best dream you've ever had?

What's the best dream you've ever had?

Conversation starters:

1. Do you have nightmares? What causes them?
2. Do you remember all your dreams?
3. Would you like to keep a dream journal?

Doodles

A drawing of my ideal life in 1 year

Draw what your dream life looks like.

A drawing of my ideal life in 3 years

MOM DOODLES

Draw what your dream life looks like.

A drawing of my ideal life in 5 years

Draw what your dream life looks like.

A drawing of my ideal life in 1 year

Draw what your dream life looks like.

A drawing of my ideal life in 3 years

DAUGHTER DOODLES

Draw what your dream life looks like.

A drawing of my ideal life in 5 years

Draw what your dream life looks like.

Bucket lists

MY BUCKET LIST
PLACES WE CAN GO TOGETHER

List out places that you'd like to travel to
together. Don't forget to set a deadline
for each item.

1

2

3

4

5

MY BUCKET LIST

THINGS WE CAN DO TOGETHER

List out some things that you'd like to do together. Don't forget to set a deadline for each item.

1

2

3

4

5

MY BUCKET LIST

MOVIES TO WATCH TOGETHER

List out some movies you'd like to watch
together. Don't forget to set a deadline
for each item.

1

2

3

4

5

Recipes to share

RECIPE CARD

RECIPE NAME

YIELD

PREP TIME

TIME TO COOK

NOTES

PROCEDURE

RECIPE CARD

RECIPE NAME

YIELD

PREP TIME

TIME TO COOK

NOTES

INGREDIENTS

PROCEDURE

RECIPE CARD

RECIPE NAME

YIELD

PREP TIME

TIME TO COOK

NOTES

PROCEDURE

RECIPE CARD

INGREDIENTS

RECIPE NAME

YIELD

PREP TIME

TIME TO COOK

NOTES

PROCEDURE

RECIPE CARD

INGREDIENTS

RECIPE NAME

YIELD

PREP TIME

TIME TO COOK

PROCEDURE

NOTES

RECIPE CARD

INGREDIENTS

RECIPE NAME

YIELD

PREP TIME

TIME TO COOK

NOTES

PROCEDURE

RECIPE CARD

INGREDIENTS

RECIPE NAME

YIELD

PREP TIME

TIME TO COOK

NOTES

PROCEDURE

RECIPE CARD

INGREDIENTS

RECIPE NAME

YIELD

PREP TIME

TIME TO COOK

NOTES

PROCEDURE

RECIPE CARD

INGREDIENTS

RECIPE NAME

YIELD

PREP TIME

TIME TO COOK

NOTES

PROCEDURE

RECIPE CARD

INGREDIENTS

RECIPE NAME

YIELD

PREP TIME

TIME TO COOK

NOTES

PROCEDURE

RECIPE CARD

RECIPE NAME

YIELD

PREP TIME

TIME TO COOK

NOTES

PROCEDURE

RECIPE CARD

INGREDIENTS

RECIPE NAME

YIELD

PREP TIME

TIME TO COOK

NOTES

PROCEDURE

letters

letters to my daughter

letters to my daughter

letters to my daughter

letters to my daughter

letters to my daughter

.

letters to my mom

Date:

:

letters to my mom

Date:

:

letters to my mom